Sports WIDOW

By Sherrie Weaver

Copyright © 1997 Great Quotations, Inc.

Cover illustration by Market Force, Burr Ridge, IL
Typography by Dmitry Feygin

Published by Great Quotations Publishing Co.,
Glendale Heights, IL

Library of Congress Catalog Number: 96-078974

ISBN 1-56245-282-7

Printed in Hong Kong

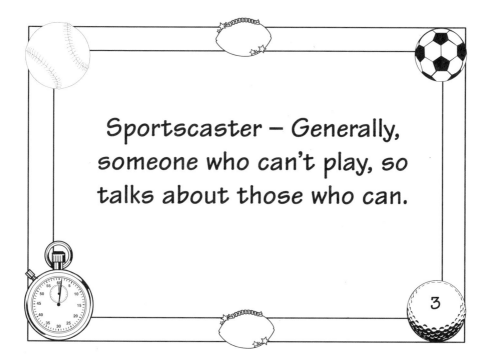

Sportscaster – Generally, someone who can't play, so talks about those who can.

3

Hockey Game – A one hour fistfight on ice, divided into periods, to better facilitate beer drinking during the event.

4

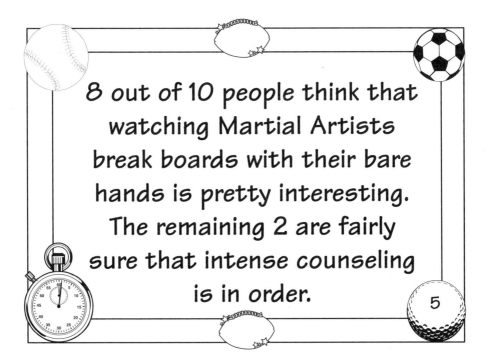

8 out of 10 people think that watching Martial Artists break boards with their bare hands is pretty interesting. The remaining 2 are fairly sure that intense counseling is in order.

5

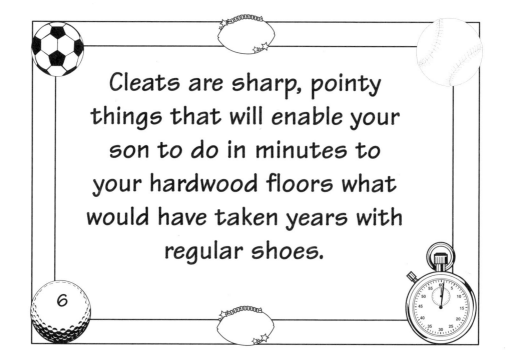

Cleats are sharp, pointy things that will enable your son to do in minutes to your hardwood floors what would have taken years with regular shoes.

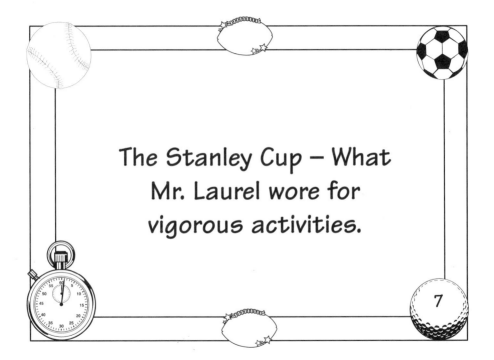

The Stanley Cup — What
Mr. Laurel wore for
vigorous activities.

7

When a guy says: "Yeah, I played some ball in college." What he probably means is: "Foosball...in the campus bar."

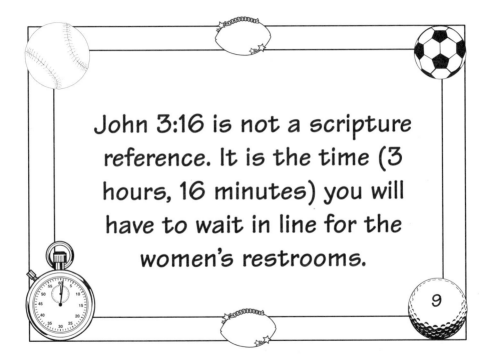

John 3:16 is not a scripture reference. It is the time (3 hours, 16 minutes) you will have to wait in line for the women's restrooms.

9

Clipping Penalty – The main
reason most football
players do not use coupons.

10

Polo – Hockey, but for people
with all their own teeth and
lots of money.

11

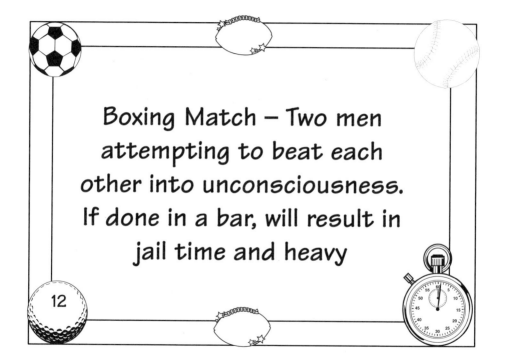

Boxing Match – Two men attempting to beat each other into unconsciousness. If done in a bar, will result in jail time and heavy

12

fines, but if done in Las Vegas, will result in huge paychecks and commercial endorsements.

13

Pinch Hitter — A girl who would rather a guy did not grab her in public.

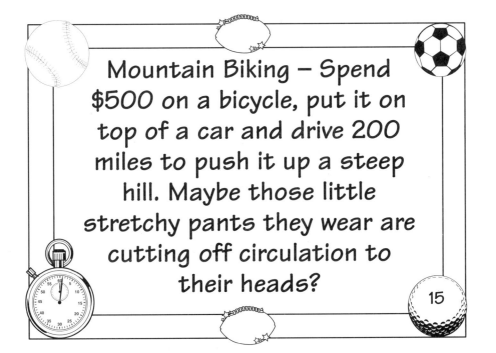

Mountain Biking – Spend $500 on a bicycle, put it on top of a car and drive 200 miles to push it up a steep hill. Maybe those little stretchy pants they wear are cutting off circulation to their heads?

15

Earned Runs – A severe
gastric disturbance, brought
on by eating way too many
'Pico De Gallo Tacos'
at "Honest Juan's
Casa de Munchies".

16

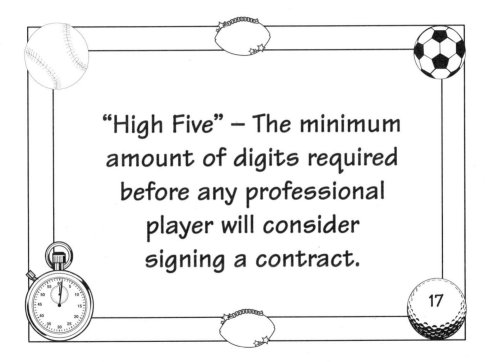

"High Five" – The minimum amount of digits required before any professional player will consider signing a contract.

17

Grand Slam – What your wife
will give the front door if
you slide into home at 3 a.m.
Especially if you bring 3
other guys with you.

18

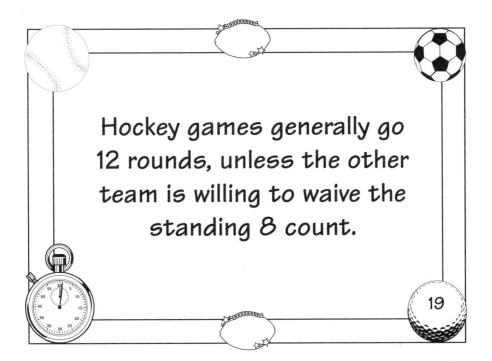

Hockey games generally go 12 rounds, unless the other team is willing to waive the standing 8 count.

19

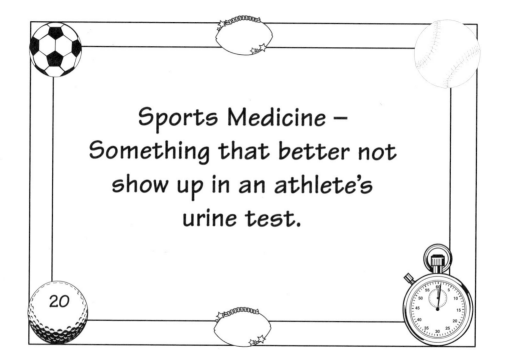

Sports Medicine –
Something that better not
show up in an athlete's
urine test.

20

Pass Interference – That blonde babe's husband showed up just as you were making your best move.

21

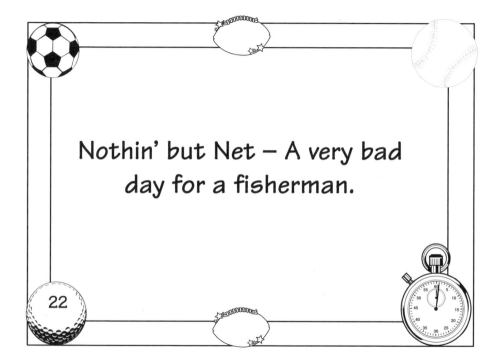

Nothin' but Net – A very bad
day for a fisherman.

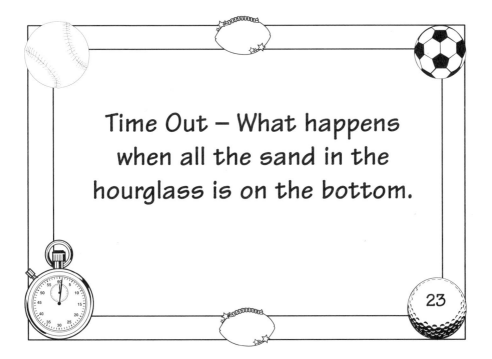

Time Out – What happens when all the sand in the hourglass is on the bottom.

23

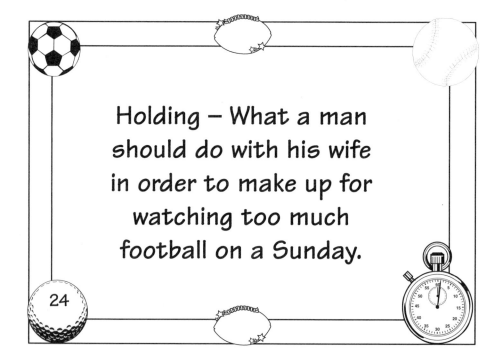

Holding – What a man should do with his wife in order to make up for watching too much football on a Sunday.

24

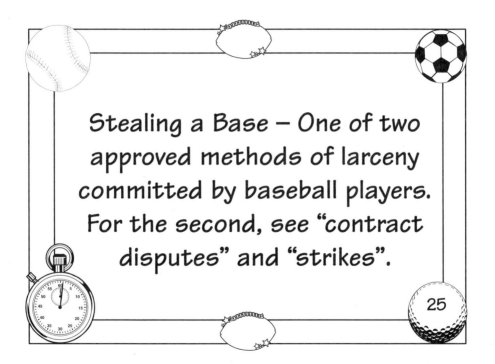

Stealing a Base – One of two approved methods of larceny committed by baseball players. For the second, see "contract disputes" and "strikes".

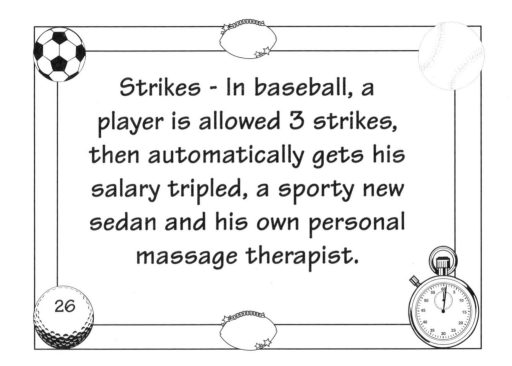

Strikes - In baseball, a player is allowed 3 strikes, then automatically gets his salary tripled, a sporty new sedan and his own personal massage therapist.

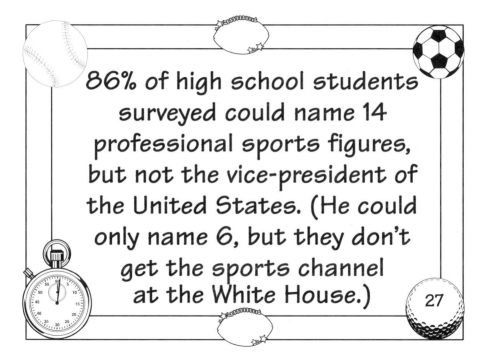

86% of high school students surveyed could name 14 professional sports figures, but not the vice-president of the United States. (He could only name 6, but they don't get the sports channel at the White House.)

27

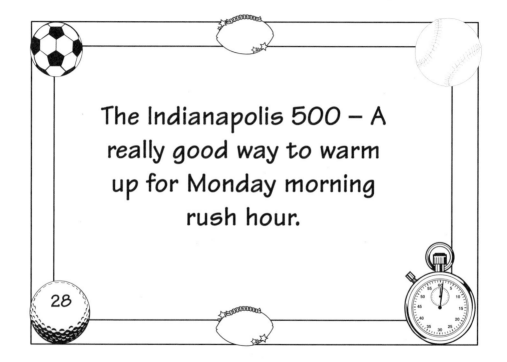

The Indianapolis 500 – A really good way to warm up for Monday morning rush hour.

28

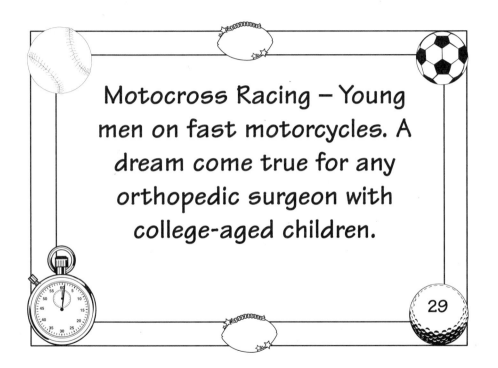

Motocross Racing – Young men on fast motorcycles. A dream come true for any orthopedic surgeon with college-aged children.

29

Season Tickets – What you'll have to do to make them taste good.

30

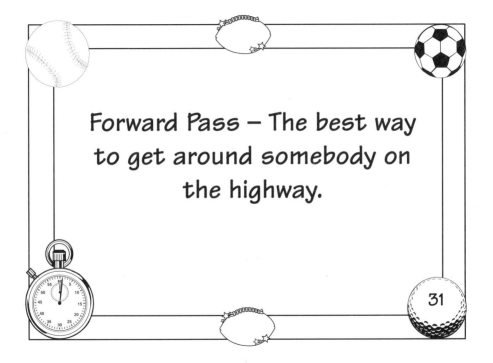

Forward Pass – The best way to get around somebody on the highway.

31

Shut Out – Where the average sporting male will find himself after spending too much time "watching the game with the guys".

32

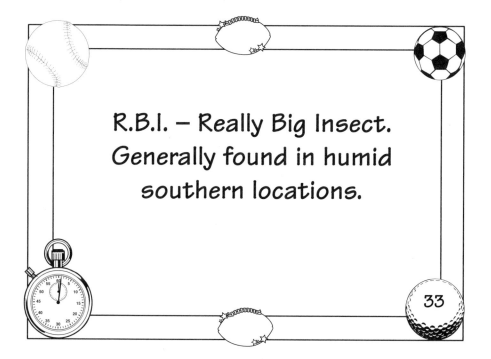

R.B.I. – Really Big Insect. Generally found in humid southern locations.

Batting Average – What really *good* hitters are doing when they're in a slump.

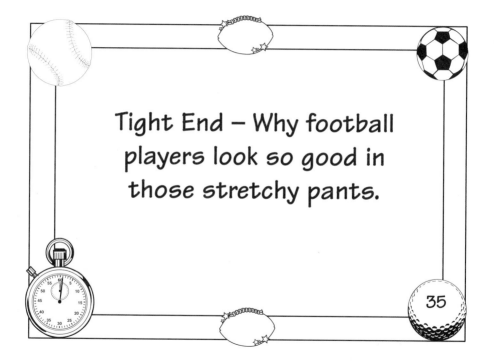

Tight End – Why football players look so good in those stretchy pants.

35

Foul Ball: 1.) One that
has been in your son's gym
bag for 4 weeks. 2.) The one
the dog has been chewing
on for 3 days.

36

Coach – A player way past
his/her prime, who was
unable to get a job
in Sportscasting.

37

"Service!" – Something Volleyball players shout when they want more coffee.

38

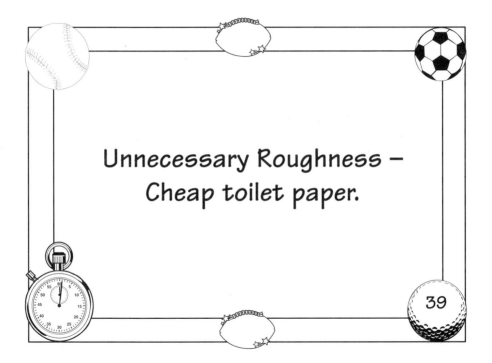

Unnecessary Roughness –
Cheap toilet paper.

39

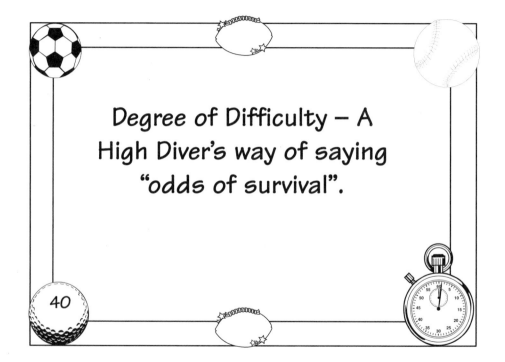

Degree of Difficulty – A High Diver's way of saying "odds of survival".

40

Fast Ball – Cinderella's party,
real quick.

41

Goalie – The only member of a Hockey Team allowed to wear protective equipment, because all the other players are trying to puck with him.

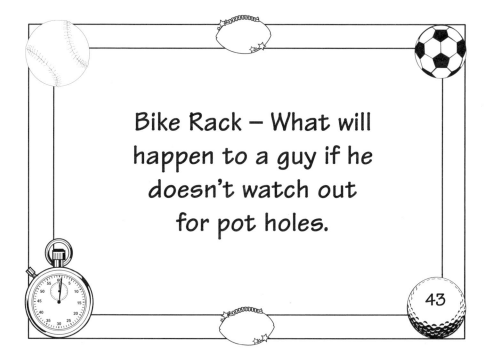

Bike Rack – What will
happen to a guy if he
doesn't watch out
for pot holes.

43

Super Bowl – Three weeks of commercialized, capitalistic, corporate sponsored feeding frenzies, capped off with a Hollywood produced

44

state-of-the-art Half Time
Show. Oh, and there's a
football game too.

60% of all baseball fans secretly believe that all those hand signals look ridiculous. 35% of the same group are pretty sure the third base coach is making them up as he goes.

46

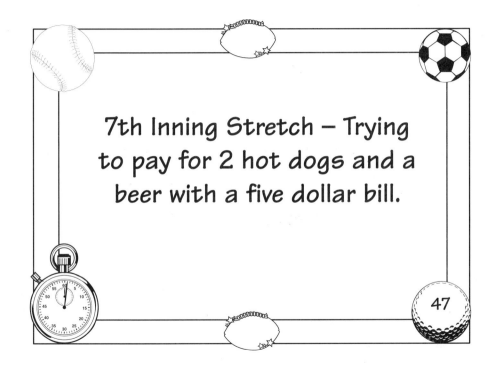

7th Inning Stretch – Trying to pay for 2 hot dogs and a beer with a five dollar bill.

Sliding Home – What you'll
have to do if you forget
to shovel the walks.

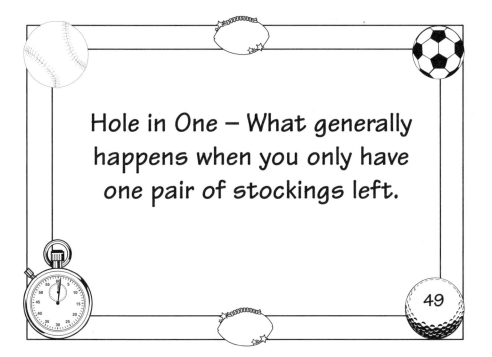

Hole in One – What generally happens when you only have one pair of stockings left.

49

If an Indy pit crew can change 4 tires, fill up a car with fuel and manage to get a drink for the driver in the span of about 12 seconds, why does the local garage still take 3 weeks to replace a door handle?

Skiing – Proof that the law of gravity is not to be trifled with.

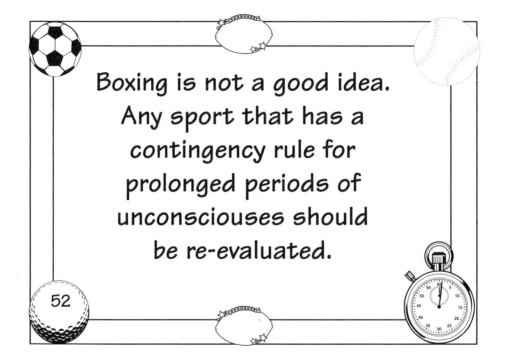

Boxing is not a good idea.
Any sport that has a
contingency rule for
prolonged periods of
unconsciouses should
be re-evaluated.

52

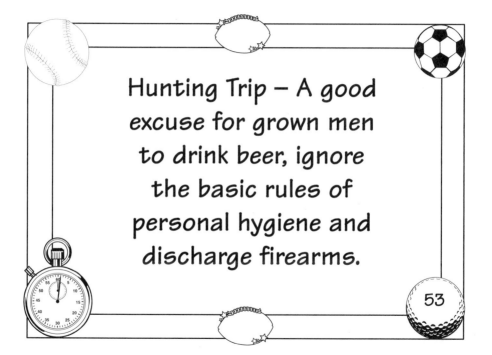

Hunting Trip – A good excuse for grown men to drink beer, ignore the basic rules of personal hygiene and discharge firearms.

53

Nice guys do not finish last.
Nice guys turn off the game
and finish the yardwork.

54

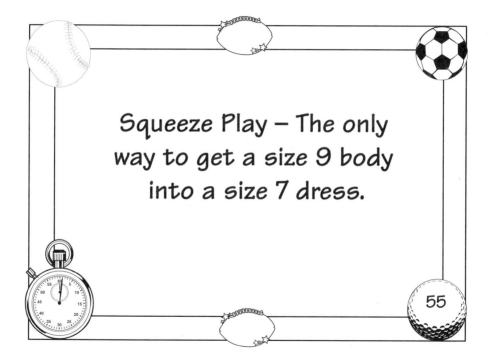

Squeeze Play – The only way to get a size 9 body into a size 7 dress.

55

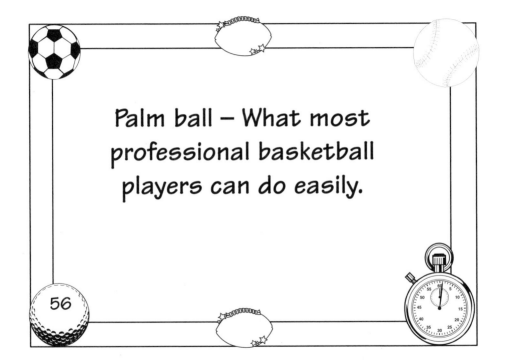

Palm ball – What most professional basketball players can do easily.

56

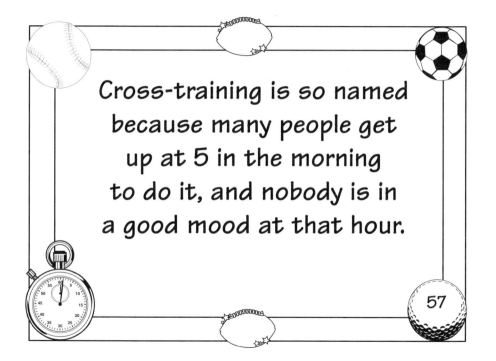

Cross-training is so named
because many people get
up at 5 in the morning
to do it, and nobody is in
a good mood at that hour.

57

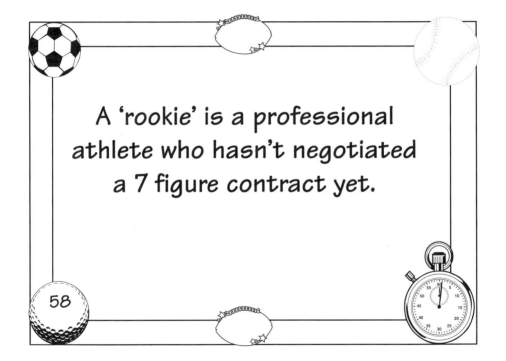

A 'rookie' is a professional athlete who hasn't negotiated a 7 figure contract yet.

58

First Round Draft - The beer you buy before you take your seat at the stadium.

59

Birdie – The bane of
car washes everywhere.

60

Dog Racing – What you'll have to do if you leave the back gate open.

61

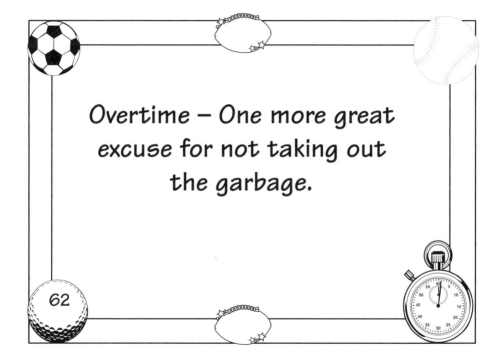

Overtime – One more great excuse for not taking out the garbage.

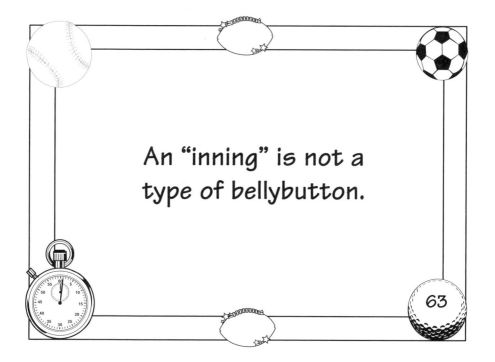

An "inning" is not a
type of bellybutton.

63

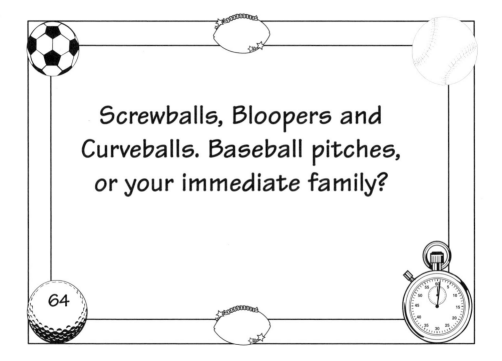

Screwballs, Bloopers and Curveballs. Baseball pitches, or your immediate family?

64

Icing – What every hockey player wants on his cake.

65

Spring Training – What you'll be doing if you buy a new puppy in April.

Team Spirit – Whatever the guys managed to smuggle into the locker room.

67

Mascot – Somebody who, for a nominal fee, puts on a giant cartoon animal suit & makes a complete fool of himself for the sake of his team.

Fan – Same thing as a mascot, except nobody gets paid.

69

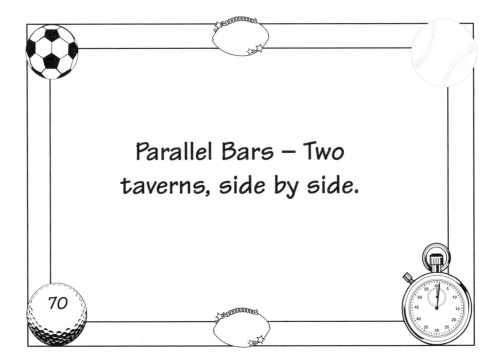

Parallel Bars – Two
taverns, side by side.

70

Rain Delay – A great excuse for stretching that "guys at the ball game" night several hours longer.

If it's called the World Series,
how come we don't ever
invite the rest of the world?

72

Checking – The main reason most hockey players pay with cash.

Ski Lodge – What your skis will probably do after you hit that tree.

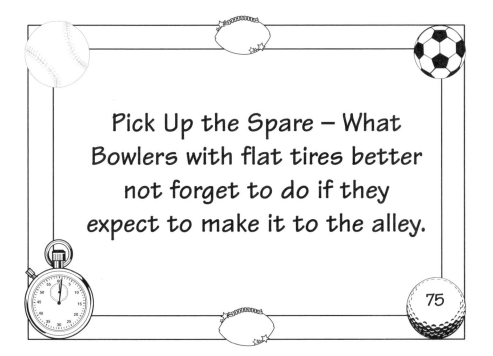

Pick Up the Spare — What Bowlers with flat tires better not forget to do if they expect to make it to the alley.

75

Fishing – Get up real early,
stand by a stream and
curse things you can't see.

76

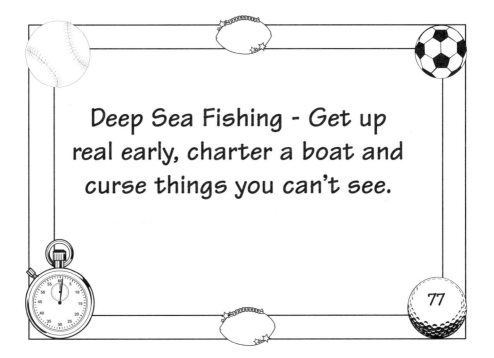

Deep Sea Fishing - Get up
real early, charter a boat and
curse things you can't see.

Dude Ranch — Like, where they grow those totally radical hombres.

Bull Pen – Where pitchers
go to talk about how
good they are.

79

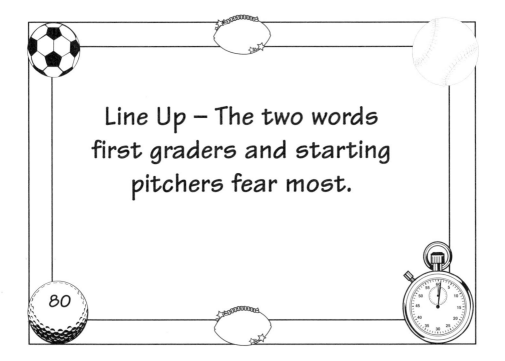

Line Up – The two words
first graders and starting
pitchers fear most.

Ringer – One who
refuses to knock.

81

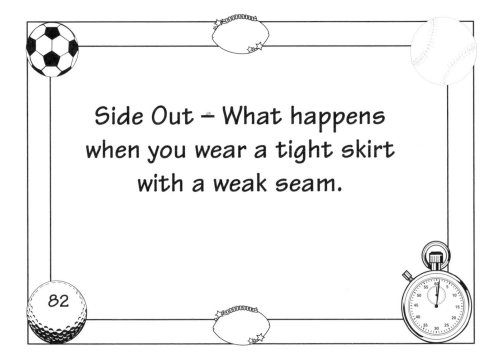

Side Out – What happens
when you wear a tight skirt
with a weak seam.

82

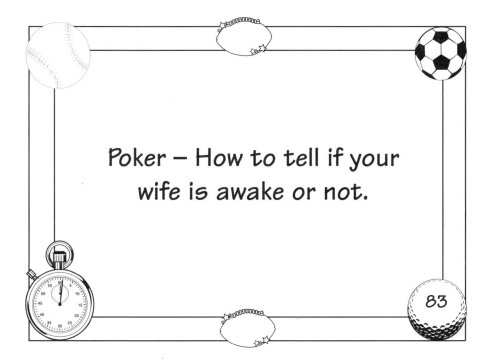

Poker – How to tell if your
wife is awake or not.

54% of all football fans believe that 'sacking the quarterback' is a good idea when his completion ratio drops drastically.

84

Safe at Home – Where you'll wish you were if it rains hard during the 3rd inning.

85

Caddy - What really good golfers get to drive.

86

Catcher's Mask – An
essential part of skin care.

87

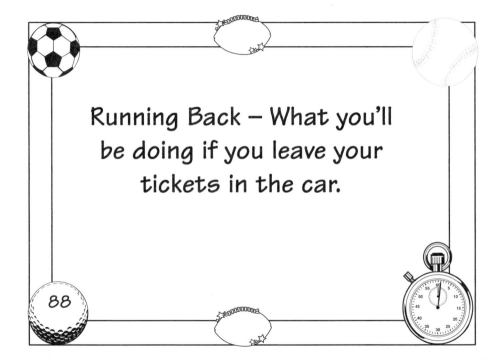

Running Back – What you'll be doing if you leave your tickets in the car.

88

Ahead in the Count – When a jock makes it all the way to 10 without using fingers.

89

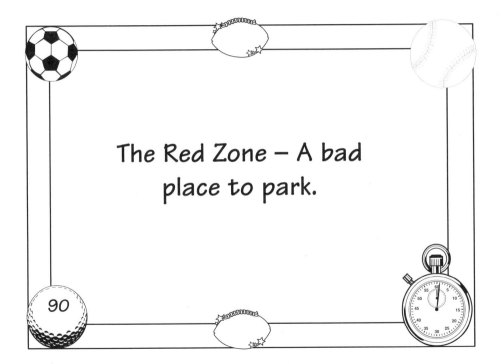

The Red Zone – A bad place to park.

90

Finish Line – Where people from Finland are forced to stand when they go to the DMV.

91

Backpacking gives men a chance to experience carrying a really heavy purse full of junk they'll never use, but don't want to be without.

Line Dancing - A large group
of people expressing their
individuality by doing the
same thing as everybody
else on the floor.

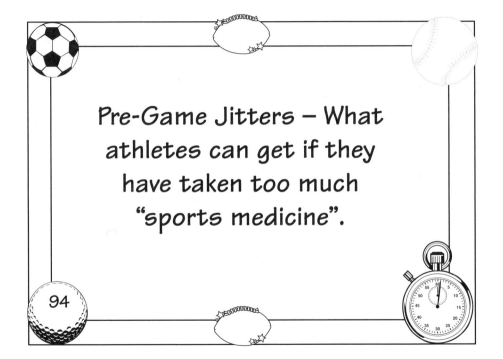

Pre-Game Jitters — What athletes can get if they have taken too much "sports medicine".

94

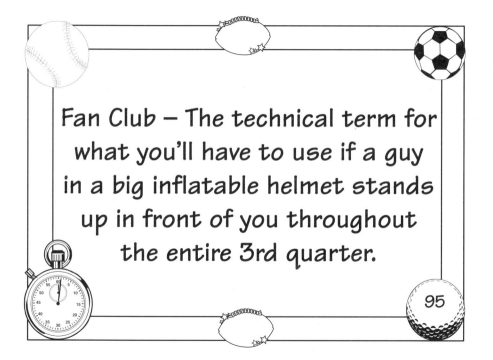

Fan Club – The technical term for what you'll have to use if a guy in a big inflatable helmet stands up in front of you throughout the entire 3rd quarter.

95

Second Quarter – The one that invariably gets stuck in the soda machine.

Wind Sprints – Hustling to the bathroom with a gut full of bad bratwurst and dark beer.

97

Bobsledding – What
kids named Robert
do every winter.

Air Ball – Somethin' the bloomin' cat will bring up, Dearie.

99

Offensive Line – "Hey, Baby, come here often?"

100

Defensive Line – "Of course
I love your new haircut."

Fullback – The kind of dress
you want your teenaged
daughter to wear to the prom.

102

Sand Trap – Tight swimming
trunks at the beach.

103

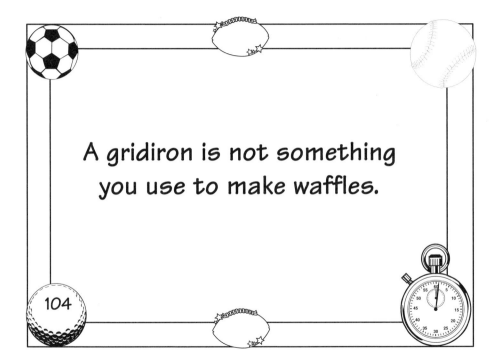

A gridiron is not something
you use to make waffles.

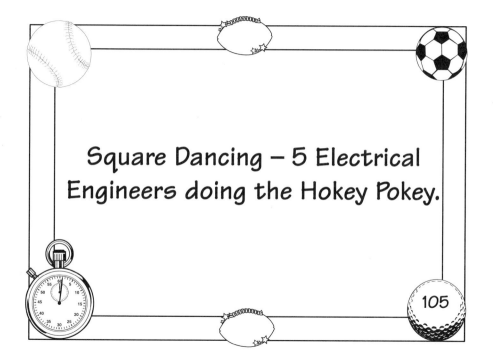

Square Dancing – 5 Electrical Engineers doing the Hokey Pokey.

End Run – The very best part of the marathon.

106

Tee Time – The best part
about British Golf.

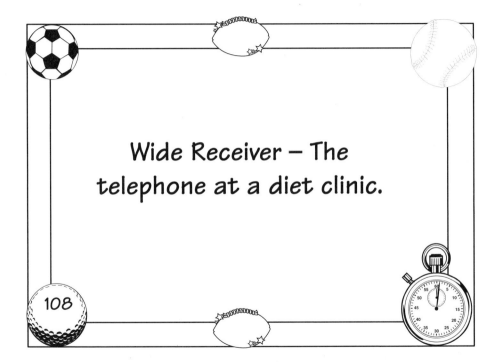

Wide Receiver – The telephone at a diet clinic.

108

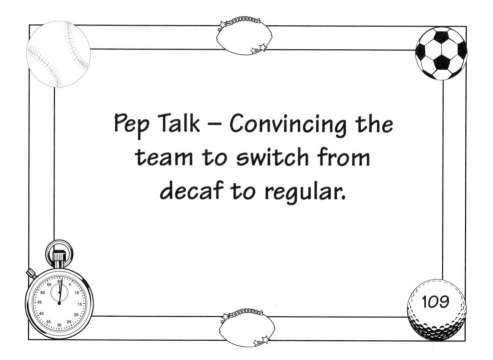

Pep Talk — Convincing the team to switch from decaf to regular.

109

Second string is a good
contingency plan for
those who frequently
break shoelaces.

Let's make golf more interesting to watch. Let's make it full contact, no pads.

111

Kentucky Derby – A stylish hat worn only in the Bluegrass state.

112

"Impressive Drive" – Austin to Fresno in a Yugo.

Bye Week – The one
right after a player is
cut from the team.

114

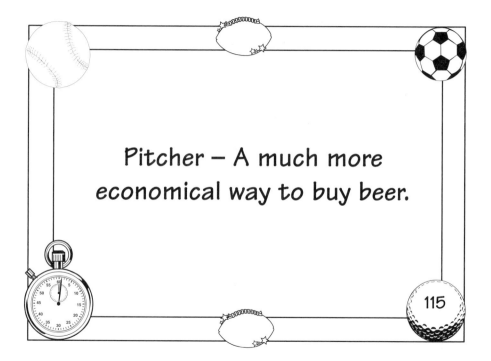

Pitcher – A much more
economical way to buy beer.

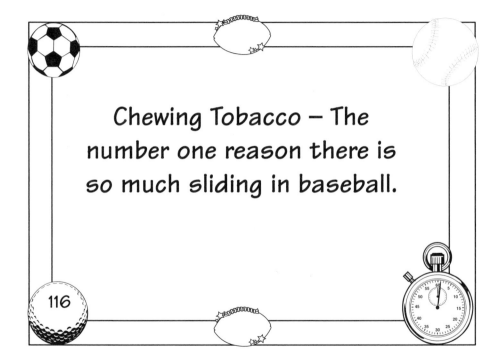

Chewing Tobacco — The number one reason there is so much sliding in baseball.

116

If you screw up in scuba diving, you get the bends. If you screw up in sky diving, you get the breaks.

What's a goalie's net worth?

118

For some hockey players,
penalties are just the icing
on the cake.

119

Remember when a "high five" was a hand gesture and not a salary?

120

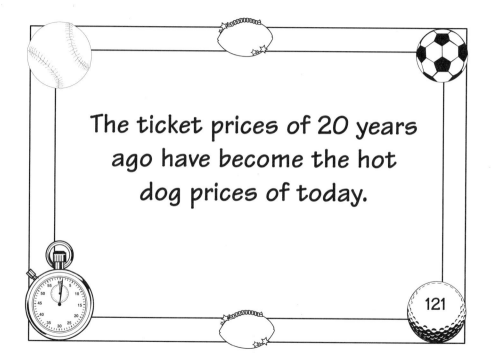

The ticket prices of 20 years ago have become the hot dog prices of today.

121

Never date divorced
basketball players. They're
all on the rebound.

122

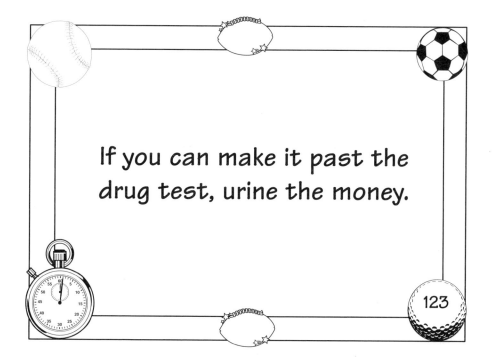

If you can make it past the drug test, urine the money.

A holdout will knock the owner's salary cap right off his head.

124

Working for a race car
driver is the pits.

125

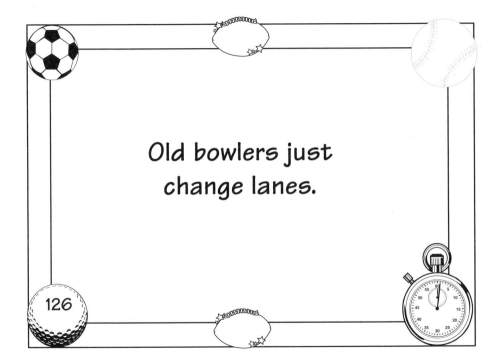

Old bowlers just
change lanes.

126

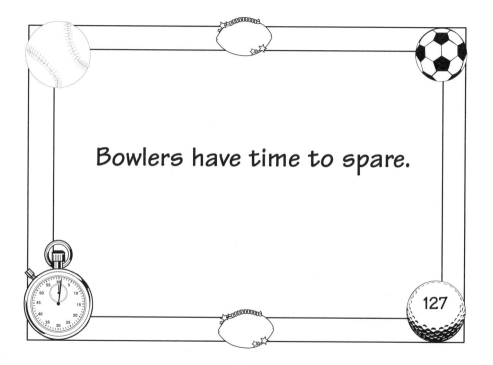

Bowlers have time to spare.

127

Pro bowlers never go on strike, but they have been known to split.

128

Retired gymnasts have been known to get broad in the beam.

Old tennis players go to seed.

130

If your father was a
taxidermist, did he ever
tan your hide?

131

Dog breeders have papers
on 'em and under 'em.

132

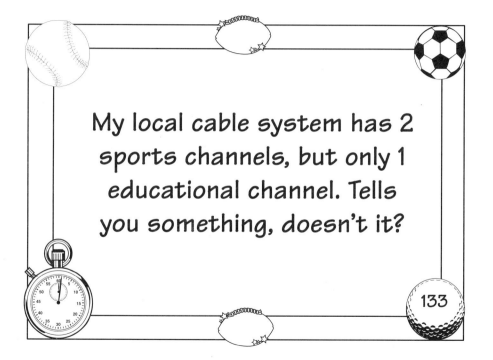

My local cable system has 2 sports channels, but only 1 educational channel. Tells you something, doesn't it?

133

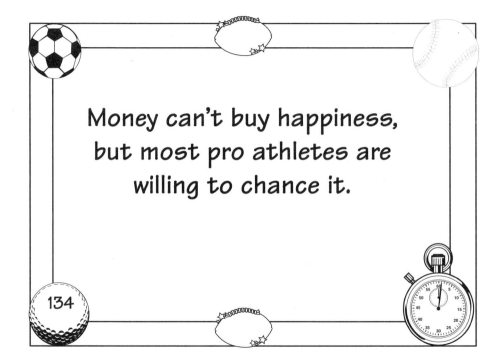

Money can't buy happiness,
but most pro athletes are
willing to chance it.

134

Scuba diving is proof
that what goes down
must come up.

135

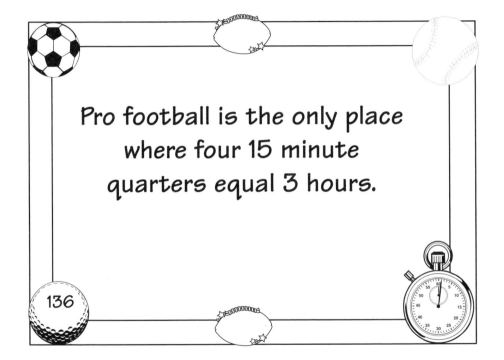

Pro football is the only place
where four 15 minute
quarters equal 3 hours.

136

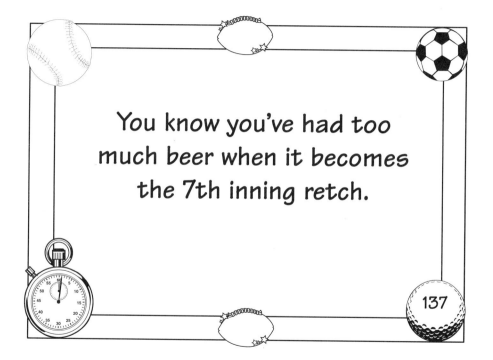

You know you've had too much beer when it becomes the 7th inning retch.

137

Linemen are so juvenile, they still play with blocks.

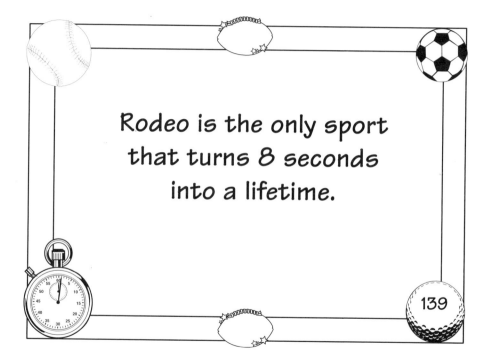

Rodeo is the only sport
that turns 8 seconds
into a lifetime.

139

Spring training puts a
bounce in an athlete's step.

It's no wonder that football
players aren't more
affectionate. If they hold
somebody, they get penalized.

141

A really good player is on the first string, a fair player is on the second string, and a mediocre player is on a shoe string.

Middle-aged folks have something in common with a winning football team. Both gain yardage in the backfield.

Professional golfers kick putt.

144

Sometimes they bogey
down, too.

145

Horseracing is the sport of kings. That's because they're the only ones who can still afford it.

146

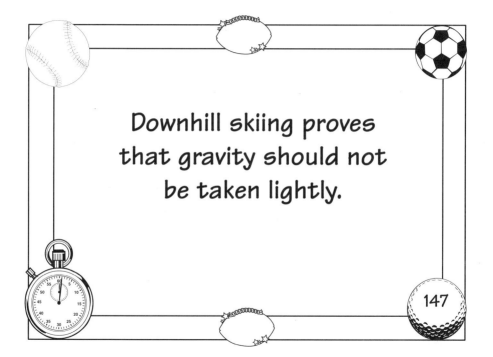

Downhill skiing proves
that gravity should not
be taken lightly.

147

Televised track events prove
that even when there is
nothing on T.V., some people
will still watch it.

148

If they're so expensive,
who do they call them
"free agents"?

Football players can't wear glasses. It's a contact sport.

150

Offensive tackle is bait
that has gone bad.

151

In some countries, grown men running ahead of a stampeding herd of bulls is a sport. In others, it's a cry for help.

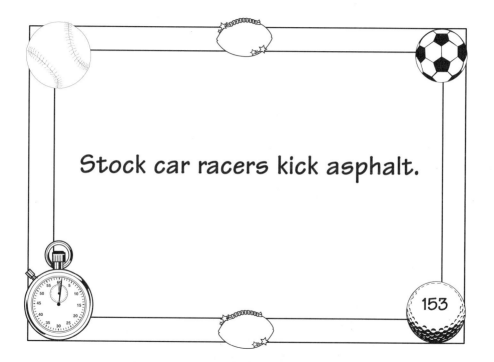

Stock car racers kick asphalt.

153

Greyhound racing is a
good example of money
going to the dogs.

154

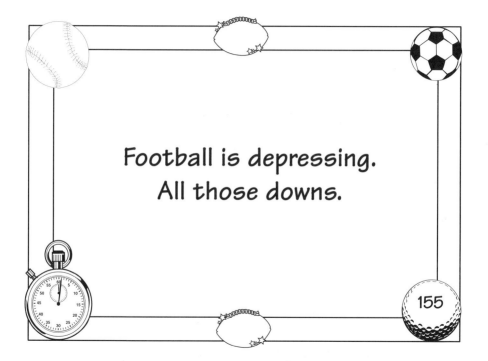

Football is depressing.
All those downs.

155

Field goal kickers do missionary work. They love conversions.

156

Good quarterbacks don't get much sleep. They hate being in the sack.

157

Mountain climbing has
it's peaks and valleys,
but no fall training.

158

In-line skating is a chance to suffer year-round the same injuries normally reserved for ice skating.

159

Quarterbacks and credit cards
are safest in the pocket.

160

Supermodels and accountants on ice: Figure skating by the numbers.

Really heavy women walking away in tight bicycling pants: Illegal motion downfield.

Rodeo riders may get roped into their jobs, but they don't take any bull.

Ten Yards to Go – Not something you want to hear if you are working for a lawn-mowing service.

When you consider the money pro basketball players make, the term "free throw" is just wishful thinking.

For white-water rafters,
life is just water under
the bridge.

166

A woman whose husband won't give up the remote: surf-bored.

167

Other Titles By Great Quotations

201 Best Things Ever Said
The ABC's of Parenting
As a Cat Thinketh
The Best of Friends
The Birthday Astrologer
Chicken Soup & Other Yiddish Say
Cornerstones of Success
Don't Deliberate ... Litigate!
Fantastic Father, Dependable Dad
Global Wisdom
Golden Years, Golden Words
Grandma, I Love You
Growing up in Toyland
Happiness is Found Along The Way
Hollywords
Hooked on Golf
In Celebration of Women
Inspirations Compelling Food for Thought
I'm Not Over the Hill
Let's Talk Decorating
Life's Lessons
Life's Simple Pleasures
A Light Heart Lives Long
Money for Nothing, Tips for Free

Mother, I Love You
Motivating Quotes for Motivated People
Mrs. Aesop's Fables
Mrs. Murphy's Laws
Mrs. Webster's Dictionary
My Daughter, My Special Friend
Other Species
Parenting 101
Reflections
Romantic Rhapsody
The Secret Language of Men
The Secret Language of Women
Some Things Never Change
The Sports Page
Sports Widow
Stress or Sanity
Teacher is Better than Two Books
Teenage of Insanity
Thanks from the Heart
Things You'll Learn if You Live Long Enough
Wedding Wonders
Working Women's World
Interior Design for Idiots
Dear Mr. President

GREAT QUOTATIONS PUBLISHING COMPANY
1967 Quincy Court
Glendale Heights, IL 60139 - 2045
Phone (630) 582-2800
Fax (630) 582- 2813